Dinosaur
Dinners

FIRST EDITION
Series Editor Deborah Lock; **Senior Editors** Shannon Beatty, Linda Esposito;
Project Editors Mary Atkinson, Caryn Jenner; **Editors** Regina Kahney, Arpita Nath;
Art Editors Karen Lieberman, Tanvi Nathyal; **Senior Art Editor** Ann Cannings;
Picture Researchers Aditya Katyal, Mary Sweeney; **Producer, Pre-Production** Marc Staples;
Senior Producer, Pre-Production Francesca Wardell; **DTP Designers** Sachin Singh, Anita Yadav;
Jacket Designers Natalie Godwin, Charlotte Jennings; **Managing Editor** Soma Chowdhury;
Deputy Managing Art Editor Jane Horne; **Managing Art Editor** Ahlawat Gunjan;
Art Director Martin Wilson; **Scientific Consultant** Dr. Angela Milner;
Reading Consultant Linda Gambrell, PhD

THIS EDITION
Editorial Management by Oriel Square
Produced for DK by WonderLab Group LLC
Jennifer Emmett, Erica Green, Kate Hale, *Founders*

Editors Grace Hill Smith, Libby Romero, Michaela Weglinski;
Photography Editors Kelley Miller, Annette Kiesow, Nicole DiMella; **Managing Editor** Rachel Houghton;
Designers Project Design Company; **Researcher** Michelle Harris; **Copy Editor** Lori Merritt;
Indexer Connie Binder; **Proofreader** Larry Shea; **Reading Specialist** Dr. Jennifer Albro;
Curriculum Specialist Elaine Larson

Published in the United States by DK Publishing
1745 Broadway, 20th Floor, New York, NY 10019

A catalog record for this book
is available from the Library of Congress.
HC ISBN: 978-0-7440-6574-9
PB ISBN: 978-0-7440-6575-6

DK books are available at special discounts when purchased
in bulk for sales promotions, premiums, fundraising, or
educational use. For details, contact: DK Publishing Special Markets,
1745 Broadway, 20th Floor, New York, NY 10019
SpecialSales@dk.com

Printed and bound in China

The publisher would like to thank the following for their kind permission to reproduce their images:
a=above; c=center; b=below; l=left; r=right; t=top; b/g=background

123RF.com: leonello calvetti 6

Cover images: *Front:* **Dorling Kindersley:** Jon Hughes br; **Dreamstime.com:** Anastasiya Aheyeva; **Getty Images / iStock:** JoeLena c

All other images © Dorling Kindersley

For the curious
www.dk.com

Dinosaur Dinners

Lee Davis

DK

Contents

See the Glossary for a guide to pronouncing dinosaur names.

What Did Dinosaurs Eat?

Different dinosaurs ate different kinds of food.

Meat Eaters

Dinosaurs that ate only meat are called carnivores.

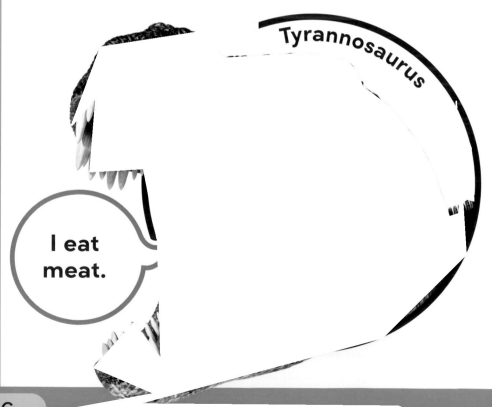

Tyrannosaurus

I eat meat.

Plant Eaters

Dinosaurs that ate only plants are called herbivores.

I eat plants.

Styracosaurus

I eat both meat and plants.

Meat and Plant Eaters

Dinosaurs that ate both meat and plants are called omnivores.

Gallimimus

Meat Eaters

Meat eaters ate fish, insects, small mammals, reptiles, and other dinosaurs.

Tyrannosaurus

Size: 37 feet (12 m) long

Feature: sharp teeth to tear meat and crush bones

Food: large dinosaurs

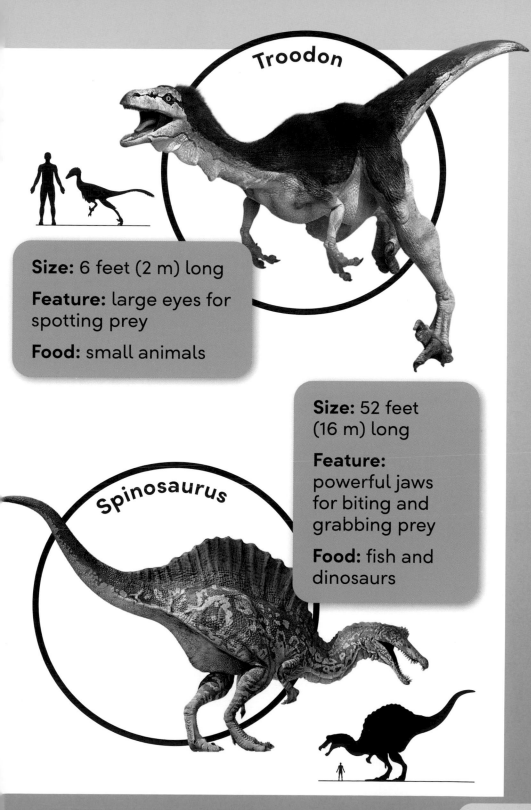

Troodon

Size: 6 feet (2 m) long

Feature: large eyes for spotting prey

Food: small animals

Spinosaurus

Size: 52 feet (16 m) long

Feature: powerful jaws for biting and grabbing prey

Food: fish and dinosaurs

I am a dinosaur
looking for my breakfast.

I have big eyes.
I can see you
wherever you are.

Troodon

I am a dinosaur
ready for my lunch.

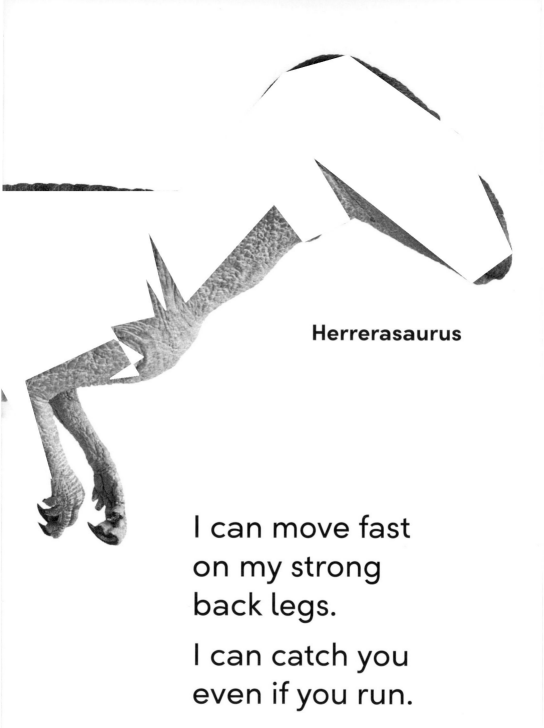

Herrerasaurus

I can move fast on my strong back legs.

I can catch you even if you run.

I am a dinosaur
hungry for my dinner.
I am bigger
than you are.

I look frightening—and I am!

Tyrannosaurus

We all have sharp
teeth and claws.
We are meat eaters.
We eat other dinosaurs.

Tyrannosaurus

Herrerasaurus

Spinosaurus

Plant Eaters

Most dinosaurs were plant eaters.
They had to watch out for meat eaters that wanted to eat them!

Barosaurus
This slow-moving dinosaur fed on all kinds of plants.

Edmontonia
This dinosaur's low-set head made it easier to eat grass.

Plateosaurus
This dinosaur stood on strong hind legs to eat leaves.

Brachiosaurus
This "gentle giant" used its long neck to reach leaves high in the trees.

I am a dinosaur
that only eats plants.
I stay close to my babies
to protect them from
meat eaters.

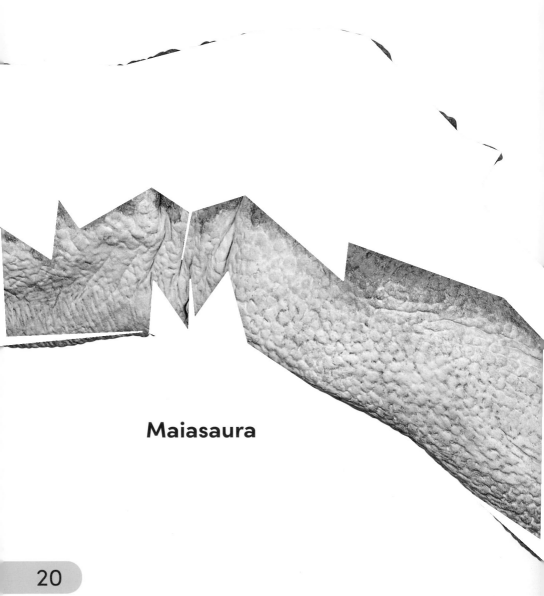

Maiasaura

I made their nest
from a mound of earth.
I bring leaves and berries
for them to eat.

We are small but fast.
We eat plants that
grow close to the ground.

Hypsilophodon

We live in a herd.
If one of us spots a meat eater,
we all zoom off on our
strong back legs.

I look frightening because
I am so big.

I need to eat huge amounts of
leaves to keep myself going.

I use my long neck
to reach the leaves
at the tops of trees.

Barosaurus

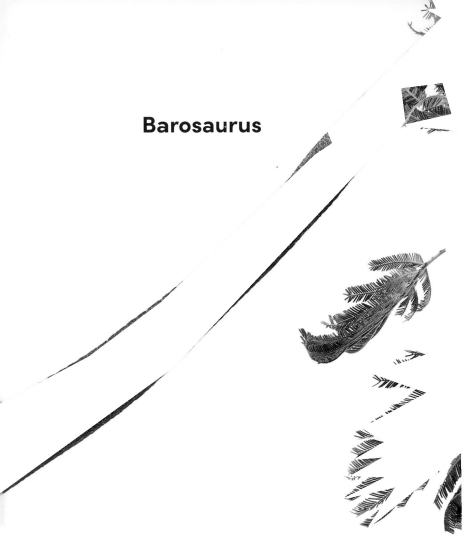

I can see danger coming
from any direction.
I am much taller than
any of the meat eaters.

We don't eat meat,
but we need protection
from dinosaurs that do!

We live in a herd and protect
each other when meat eaters
come too close.

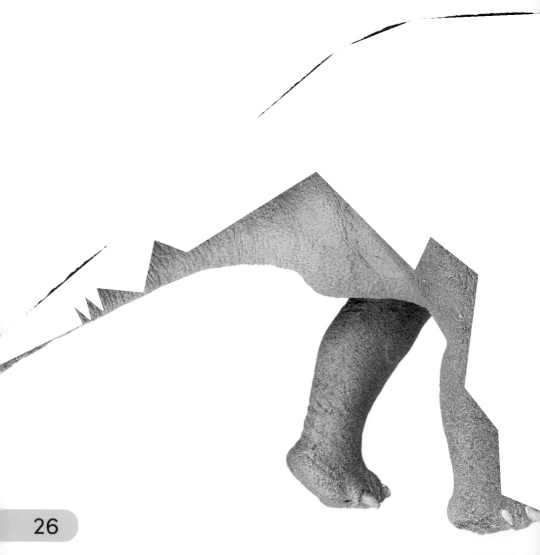

Styracosaurus

I protect myself.
Sharp teeth cannot dent
my body armor.

I may move slowly, but
watch out for the spikes
on my shoulders.

Edmontonia

Glossary

Barosaurus
(BAR-oh-sore-us)
A dinosaur that ate plants. Its name means "heavy lizard."

Brachiosaurus
(BRAK-ee-oh-SORE-us)
A dinosaur that ate plants. Its name means "arm lizard."

Edmontonia
(ed-mon-TONE-ee-ah)
A dinosaur that ate plants. Its name means "from Edmonton" (Canada).

Gallimimus
(GAL-uh-MY-mus)
A dinosaur that ate plants and animals. Its name means "imitator."

Herrerasaurus
(herr-ray-rah-SORE-us)
A dinosaur that ate animals.
It is named after Victorino Herrera, who discovered it.

Hypsilophodon
(hip-sih-LOH-foh-don)
A dinosaur that ate plants. Its name means "high ridge tooth."

Maiasaura
(my-ah-SORE-ah)
A dinosaur that ate plants. Its name means "good mother lizard."

Plateosaurus
(plat-ee-oh-SORE-us)
A dinosaur that ate plants. Its name means "flat lizard."

Spinosaurus
(SPINE-oh-SORE-us)
A dinosaur that ate animals. Its name means "thorn lizard."

Styracosaurus
(sty-RAK-oh-sore-us)
A dinosaur that ate plants. Its name means "spiked lizard."

Troodon
(TROH-oh-don)
A dinosaur that ate animals. Its name means "wounding tooth."

Tyrannosaurus
(tie-RAN-oh-SORE-us)
A dinosaur that ate animals. Its name means "tyrant lizard."

Index

Quiz

Answer the questions to see what you have learned. Check your answers in the key below.

Which dinosaur am I?

1. I live in big herds that protect me from meat eaters.

2. I run very fast. I use my sharp claws when I hunt for meat.

3. I use my sharp teeth to tear meat and crush the bones of other large dinosaurs.

4. I move slowly and eat many kinds of plants.

5. I eat both plants and animals.

1. Styracosaurus 2. Herrerasaurus 3. Tyrannosaurus
4. Barosaurus 5. Gallimimus